CONTENTS

SOUTH KOREA UNLOCKED: A SHORT GUIDE TO TRAVELLING AND SELLING IN SOUTH KOREA

JK Lewis

Introduction

South Korea is a fascinating blend of tradition and modernity, where ancient palaces and temples coexist with skyscrapers and tech hubs. Known for its advanced technology, vibrant pop culture, and trendsetting influence, South Korea has emerged as one of Asia's most dynamic markets. For entrepreneurs, South Korea offers a unique opportunity to tap into a highly connected, trend-sensitive, and digitally savvy consumer base. With a population that values quality, innovation, and brand integrity, the South Korean market is competitive but full of potential.

This guide will take you through everything you need to know about travelling, selling, and succeeding in South Korea. Whether you're interested in selling industrial equipment, traditional crafts in bustling markets, introducing new tech products online, or setting up long-term business partnerships, understanding South Korea's distinct consumer culture and business etiquette will give you the tools to stand out in this competitive environment.

Why South Korea?

South Korea's economy is among the top 10 globally, driven by industries ranging from technology and automotive to beauty and fashion. The country's consumers are some of the most digitally engaged in the world, with a keen interest in innovation, quality, and sustainability. South Korea's online retail landscape is also one of the fastest-growing, making it a prime market for entrepreneurs looking to reach tech-savvy and trend-conscious consumers.

The country's influence, particularly in entertainment and fashion, extends beyond its borders. South Korea's pop culture wave, known as Hallyu, has spread worldwide through K-pop, K-dramas, and beauty trends, creating international demand for Korean products and an increased openness to foreign brands that align with Korean tastes.

What You'll Learn

In this guide, we will explore each aspect of travelling, selling, and building a business in South Korea, providing the insights and strategies you need to thrive in this unique market. We'll cover:

- Understanding South Korean culture and consumer behaviour: Learn how regional differences, cultural values, and the country's fast-moving trends influence buying decisions across South Korea.

- Travelling and logistics: Discover South Korea's modern, efficient transport system, the best options for business travellers, and tips for managing your inventory, shipping, and delivery efficiently.

- Setting up your business: From choosing the right business structure to understanding taxes and consumer protection laws, we'll guide you through the steps for establishing your business in South Korea.

- Selling Industrial products and services: South Korea is a competitive and advanced market, you'll gain a deep understanding of local industry demands, regulatory compliance, and a commitment to quality and innovation.

- Selling at markets and fairs: Whether in Seoul's bustling markets or local fairs, this section covers how to apply for a stall, create an attractive setup, and connect with customers directly.

- Building a strong online presence: South Korea's online and mobile-first market is one of the world's most advanced. Learn how to optimise your website, choose the best e-commerce platforms, and tailor your digital marketing strategy for South Korean consumers.

- Effective marketing strategies: Explore how to reach South Korean consumers through social media, influencer marketing, and localised content. Discover how South Korean culture, particularly K-pop and digital trends, can amplify your marketing efforts.

- Navigating South Korean business etiquette: Business interactions in South Korea are shaped by respect for hierarchy, formality, and long-term relationships. Understanding the subtleties of South Korean business culture is essential for building trust and credibility with clients and partners.

Opportunities and Challenges

South Korea's market presents a wealth of opportunities, but it also requires adaptability and sensitivity to local customs. Consumers here expect high standards of quality, are quick to adopt new trends, and appreciate brands that align with their values. The market's rapid pace means that brands must stay agile, innovative, and ready to evolve to meet changing demands. Success in South Korea hinges on cultural understanding, the ability to engage with a trend-driven market, and a commitment to quality and professionalism.

Embrace the Opportunity

South Korea is a vibrant, competitive market that rewards brands willing to adapt to its unique consumer culture and fast-paced environment. By leveraging this guide, you'll gain the insights, tools, and strategies needed to navigate South Korea with confidence, whether you're establishing your brand online, setting up a stall in a local market, or engaging in long-term business partnerships. As you embark on this journey, remember that adaptability, respect for cultural nuances, and a focus on quality are your keys to unlocking success in South Korea.

CHAPTER 1: THE GEOGRAPHY AND CULTURE OF SOUTH KOREA

South Korea's culture is a unique mix of modern innovation and deeply rooted tradition. The country's landscape is as varied as its culture, from bustling urban centres like Seoul to serene rural areas where traditional practices and values are upheld. Understanding the distinct characteristics of South Korea's regions and the influences that shape consumer behaviour is essential for successfully navigating this dynamic market.

In this chapter, we'll explore South Korea's regional diversity, the differences between urban and rural markets, and the cultural values that guide consumer decisions.

1.1 Overview of South Korea's Regions

South Korea is divided into several regions, each with its own cultural identity, economic strengths, and consumer preferences. From the technology-driven heart of Seoul to the coastal city of Busan and the countryside, each area offers distinct opportunities and challenges for businesses.

Seoul – The Capital and Economic Powerhouse

- **Overview**: Seoul is South Korea's largest city and the centre of the nation's economy, culture, and politics. It's one of the most technologically advanced cities in the world, with a fast-paced consumer market that values innovation, convenience, and quality.

- **Key Industries**: Technology, finance, fashion, and beauty are major industries in Seoul. The city is known for its role in the global rise of K-beauty, K-pop, and cutting-edge tech.

- **Consumer Preferences**: Seoul consumers are trend-focused and brand-conscious. They appreciate premium and luxury products, particularly those with a strong online presence or association with celebrities or influencers. Green and eco-friendly products are also popular, especially among younger consumers.

Busan – South Korea's Gateway to the Sea

- **Overview**: Located on the southeastern coast, Busan is South Korea's second-largest city and one of Asia's busiest ports. Known for its scenic beaches, film festivals, and cultural heritage, Busan attracts both local and international visitors.

- **Key Industries**: Port and logistics, tourism, and food and beverage. Busan is famous for its seafood and local specialities.

- **Consumer Preferences**: Compared to Seoul, Busan has a slightly slower pace, with consumers focused on local products and unique items that reflect the city's maritime culture. Traditional markets play a significant role in Busan, and there is a growing interest in lifestyle and wellness products.

Daegu – The Textile and Fashion Hub

- **Overview**: Known as the "Textile City," Daegu has a rich history in the textile and fashion industries. The city is also developing as a centre for medical tourism, thanks to its focus on healthcare and wellness.

- **Key Industries**: Textiles, fashion, healthcare, and medical tourism.

- **Consumer Preferences**: Daegu consumers often seek stylish, high-quality fashion and lifestyle products, and the city's reputation for healthcare and wellness has created a strong market for health-conscious and beauty products.

Other Cities – Daejeon, Gwangju, and Jeju Island

- **Daejeon**: Known as South Korea's "Silicon Valley," Daejeon is a hub for technology and research. It's home to numerous research institutes and tech start-ups, making it an ideal market for tech-related products and innovation.

- **Gwangju**: A city rich in history and art, Gwangju has a strong cultural identity. The city hosts art festivals and attracts a creative consumer base interested in culture, design, and traditional products.

- **Jeju Island**: A popular tourist destination, Jeju Island is known for its natural beauty, eco-tourism, and unique local products, such as Jeju tea and volcanic skincare. The island's focus on sustainability and tourism offers a niche market for eco-friendly and local products.

1.2 Urban vs. Rural Markets

Understanding the differences between South Korea's urban and rural markets is essential for tailoring your business strategy. While urban areas offer a fast-paced consumer base eager for innovation and trends, rural regions maintain a slower pace with a focus on traditional values and community.

Urban Markets

- **Key Characteristics**: South Korea's urban centres, particularly Seoul and Busan, are highly connected, trend-sensitive, and brand-conscious. Consumers in these areas are accustomed to fast fashion, rapid delivery services, and digital innovation. They are open to new products and trends, particularly those promoted by influencers or associated with popular culture.

- **What Sells**: Premium products, cutting-edge technology, fashion, beauty, and lifestyle products perform well in urban markets. Products that emphasise convenience, quality, and innovation resonate strongly with urban consumers.

Rural Markets

- **Key Characteristics**: Rural areas in South Korea have a slower pace, with strong community ties and a greater focus on traditional values. Consumers in these areas are more likely to support local businesses and seek out products with a connection to the area's heritage or culture.

- **What Sells**: Traditional crafts, local food products, and sustainable goods are popular in rural markets. Items associated with South Korean culture or local customs, such as pottery, textiles, and natural skincare, tend to perform well.

1.3 Understanding South Korean Consumer Culture

South Korean consumers are highly trend-sensitive, digitally engaged, and quality-conscious. Consumer preferences in South Korea are heavily influenced by pop culture, technology, and a strong appreciation for aesthetics. Below are some of the core values that shape South Korean consumer behaviour.

Influence of Hallyu (Korean Wave)

The global phenomenon of Hallyu, or the "Korean Wave," has made South Korean music, television, and fashion popular worldwide. This influence is just as strong domestically, where K-pop stars, actors, and influencers play a significant role in shaping consumer trends. Endorsements from celebrities, collaborations with K-pop stars, and products that align with popular culture can significantly boost brand appeal.

- **Key Insight**: Brands that align with K-pop or Korean drama trends, or that partner with South Korean influencers, can gain substantial visibility and credibility among consumers.

Digital Engagement and Technology

South Korea is one of the world's most digitally connected countries, with some of the highest internet and smartphone penetration rates globally. South Korean consumers are accustomed to shopping online, engaging with brands through social media, and using digital payment systems.

- **Key Insight**: A strong digital presence is essential in South Korea. Consumers expect easy access to products online, seamless payment options, and responsive customer service. E-commerce, m-commerce (mobile commerce), and live shopping are popular, especially for beauty and fashion products.

Quality and Brand Loyalty

South Korean consumers value quality and often develop strong loyalty to brands that meet their expectations. Reputation and perceived quality are important, especially for products related to health, beauty, and technology. South Korean consumers are also highly informed, frequently researching products and reading reviews before purchasing.

- **Key Insight**: Building brand loyalty in South Korea requires consistently high-quality products, transparent branding, and excellent customer service. Many consumers prefer established brands, but newer brands that offer quality and unique appeal can still gain traction.

Sustainability and Ethical Consumption

While South Korea's emphasis on sustainability is relatively recent, it is growing rapidly, particularly among younger consumers. Eco-friendly products, ethical sourcing, and minimal packaging are increasingly valued. Brands that highlight their commitment to sustainability can appeal to this growing demand.

- **Key Insight**: Products with eco-friendly packaging, cruelty-free certifications, or sustainable sourcing are becoming more popular, especially in the beauty, fashion, and food sectors. Positioning your brand as eco-conscious can help you appeal to environmentally aware consumers.

Aesthetics and Design

In South Korea, aesthetics play a significant role in consumer choices. From product packaging to store layout and online presence, South Korean consumers appreciate visually appealing, well-designed products. Minimalism, elegance, and attention to detail are highly valued, especially in the beauty and lifestyle markets.

- **Key Insight**: Invest in appealing packaging and visually attractive marketing materials. Whether online or in-store, aesthetics can make a strong impression and help differentiate your brand.

Chapter 1 - Summary

Understanding the diverse regions, urban-rural dynamics, and unique cultural influences in South Korea is essential to connecting with South Korean consumers. From Seoul's fast-paced, trend-driven market to the traditional and community-oriented values of rural areas, South Korea offers a complex but rewarding market landscape. South Korean consumers are discerning, brand-loyal, and digitally engaged, making it crucial for businesses to align with their preferences and values. By considering regional characteristics, embracing the influence of Hallyu culture, and prioritising quality and aesthetics, you can position your brand for success in South Korea.

CHAPTER 2: THE LOGISTICS OF TRAVELLING IN SOUTH KOREA

South Korea's advanced infrastructure and highly efficient public transport system make it one of the easiest countries in Asia for business travel. Whether you're attending meetings in Seoul, selling at markets in Busan, or exploring smaller cities, South Korea offers a range of convenient transportation options to get you there quickly and comfortably. This chapter will guide you through the essentials of travelling within South Korea, including transport options, business accommodation, and tips for organising the transport of goods.

2.1 Transportation Options

South Korea's transport network is among the most efficient in the world, covering everything from bullet trains and subways to buses and domestic flights, alongside a high-quality road network. Choosing the right option depends on your destination, budget, and time constraints.

Public Transport: Efficient and Reliable

South Korea's public transport system is highly developed, especially in urban centres like Seoul, Busan, and Daegu. With punctual services, affordable fares, and extensive coverage, public transport is often the best option for business travellers.

- **Subway**: The subway systems in cities like Seoul, Busan, and Daegu are clean, affordable, and extensive. The Seoul Metro, for example, has one of the longest networks in the world and offers easy access to nearly every part of the city.
    - **T-Money Card**: The T-Money card is a reloadable transport card that works across

subways, buses, and even some taxis. It's highly recommended for convenience, as it also allows transfers between different forms of public transport.

- ◦ **English-Friendly**: Subway stations and trains in major cities provide signs and announcements in English, making it easy for international travellers to navigate.

- **Buses**: South Korea's bus system includes both local and intercity services, making it possible to travel between cities or within specific neighbourhoods.
  - ◦ **Express Buses**: For long-distance travel between cities, express buses are comfortable and affordable. Major terminals like **Seoul Express Bus Terminal** offer services to almost every city in the country.
  - ◦ **Convenience**: Buses are a great option for areas not covered by the subway and are often equipped with Wi-Fi, USB charging ports, and comfortable seating.

KTX (Korea Train Express): High-Speed Rail

South Korea's high-speed rail, the KTX, is a fast and reliable way to travel between cities. With speeds of up to 300 km/h, it significantly reduces travel time, making it ideal for business trips.

- **Routes and Destinations**: The KTX connects Seoul with major cities like Busan, Daejeon, and Gwangju. The journey from Seoul to Busan, for instance, takes approximately 2.5 hours, making day trips between cities feasible.

- **Booking Tickets**: Tickets can be booked online or at train stations, and discounts are often available for early bookings or group travel.

- **KORAIL Pass**: For travellers who plan to make multiple train journeys, this pass offers unlimited travel on the KTX and other Korean trains for a set period, which can be more economical.

Car Rentals: Flexibility for Reaching Remote Areas

While public transport is usually sufficient, renting a car can offer additional flexibility, particularly if you're travelling to remote areas or carrying a large amount of inventory.

- **Rental Process**: Car rental agencies are available at major airports and in larger cities. Foreigners can rent a car with an **International Driving Permit (IDP)**, which must be carried alongside a valid driving licence.

- **Traffic and Navigation**: South Korea's roads are well-maintained, but traffic in major cities can be heavy. GPS navigation is essential, and many rental agencies offer English GPS or mobile navigation apps like **Naver Map** or **KakaoMap**, which support English-language navigation.

Domestic Flights

For longer journeys, such as from Seoul to Jeju Island, domestic flights are the quickest option. South Korea has several budget airlines, including **Jeju Air**, **Air Busan**, and **Jin Air**, which offer affordable flights between cities.

- **Convenience**: Domestic flights are frequent and reliable, with short check-in times. For travel to Jeju Island, flights are generally more convenient and faster than ferries.

2.2 Accommodation for Business Travellers

South Korea offers a wide range of accommodation options to suit different budgets and preferences, from business hotels and serviced apartments to traditional guesthouses. Choosing the right accommodation can make your trip more productive and comfortable.

Business Hotels

Business hotels are widely available in major cities and are tailored to meet the needs of professionals, offering amenities like free Wi-Fi, work desks, meeting rooms, and business centres.

- **Examples**: Chains like **Lotte City Hotels**, **Shilla Stay**, and **Novotel** have multiple locations across the country, providing a high standard of comfort and service for business travellers.

- **Key Areas**: In Seoul, popular business districts for hotels include **Gangnam**, **Jongno**, and **Myeong-dong**, while in Busan, **Haeundae** and **Seomyeon** offer convenient options.

Serviced Apartments and Short-Term Rentals

For longer stays or if you need more space, serviced apartments or short-term rentals can provide a home-like environment with added flexibility.

- **Serviced Apartments**: Providers like **Oakwood Premier** and **Fraser Place** offer serviced apartments with kitchen facilities, laundry, and additional amenities, ideal for extended business trips.

- **Airbnb and Local Alternatives**: Short-term rentals through **Airbnb** or Korean platforms like **Zigbang** are also popular, particularly for travellers who prefer a more local experience or require extra space for inventory.

Traditional Guesthouses (Hanok Stays)

For a unique experience, consider staying in a **hanok** guesthouse. Hanoks are traditional Korean houses that offer a blend of culture and comfort. They are ideal for shorter stays, especially if you're travelling to regions known for their cultural heritage, like **Bukchon Hanok Village** in Seoul or **Gyeongju**.

2.3 Organising the Transport of Goods

If you're bringing goods into South Korea or need to transport inventory between cities, understanding the local shipping and logistics options is essential for smooth operations.

International Shipping and Customs

When importing goods to South Korea, it's crucial to navigate customs and import regulations.

- **Customs and Documentation**: South Korea has strict import regulations, so be prepared with all necessary documentation, including invoices, certificates of origin, and product descriptions.

- **Import Duties**: South Korea imposes tariffs on certain imported goods, so check if your products fall under any duty exemptions or reductions. Customs brokers can assist with the clearance process, helping to avoid delays.

Domestic Shipping and Couriers

South Korea has a variety of domestic shipping options, from express couriers to standard parcel services, making it easy to deliver goods to customers or transport inventory between locations.

- **Korea Post**: The national postal service, **Korea Post**, offers reliable domestic and international shipping options at competitive rates. It's ideal for small parcels and regular business shipping needs.

- **Private Couriers**: **CJ Logistics**, **Hanjin Express**, and **Lotte Global Logistics** are some of South Korea's leading private couriers, offering express and same-day delivery options for both domestic and international shipments.

Click-and-Collect Services

For e-commerce businesses, offering click-and-collect options is popular in South Korea, as consumers value flexibility and convenience.

- **Convenience Store Pick-Up**: South Korea's convenience stores, including **CU** and **GS25**, often act as pick-up points for online orders. This can be a convenient option for customers and is well-suited to smaller products or parcels.

- **Delivery to Locker Services**: Self-service delivery lockers are widely available in cities and are an increasingly popular choice for customers. These lockers, offered by companies like **Boxful** and **Pick-up Service**, allow customers to collect their packages at a time that suits them.

Chapter 2 - Summary

South Korea's world-class transport and logistics systems make it easy to travel between cities, manage inventory, and deliver products to customers efficiently. Whether you're navigating Seoul's subway system, taking the KTX to Busan, or organising deliveries via domestic couriers, South Korea offers a range of reliable options for business travellers. By planning your accommodation and logistics carefully, you can ensure that your time in South Korea is both productive and convenient, setting you up for success in this dynamic market.

CHAPTER 3: SETTING UP YOUR BUSINESS IN SOUTH KOREA

Starting a business in South Korea can be a straightforward process if you understand the local legal and regulatory requirements. South Korea has a business-friendly environment, especially for foreign entrepreneurs and small to medium enterprises. However, compliance with local tax obligations, choosing the right business structure, and understanding consumer protection laws are essential for establishing a successful operation in the South Korean market.

In this chapter, we'll guide you through choosing the right business structure, registering your company, managing taxes, and ensuring compliance with South Korean regulations.

3.1 Choosing Your Business Structure

Selecting the correct business structure is crucial, as it will affect your tax obligations, administrative responsibilities, and legal requirements. South Korea offers several business structures for foreign entrepreneurs and companies.

Sole Proprietorship

A **sole proprietorship** is the simplest business structure, often chosen by small, independent business owners. This structure requires minimal administrative responsibilities and is straightforward to set up.

- **Advantages**: Simple registration process, minimal paperwork, and direct control over the business.
- **Disadvantages**: Personal liability for business debts, meaning your personal assets are at risk.
- **Registration**: To register as a sole proprietor, you must

visit your local **District Tax Office** and complete the necessary tax registration. You'll also need a **business registration certificate**, which is required for all commercial activities in South Korea.

Limited Liability Company (Yuhan Hoesa)

A **Yuhan Hoesa**, or Limited Liability Company (LLC), is a common structure for small to medium-sized businesses. It provides limited liability, meaning your personal assets are protected, and is suitable for businesses looking to expand and employ local staff.

- **Advantages**: Limited liability for owners, easier to raise capital, and more credibility with partners and clients.
- **Disadvantages**: Higher administrative requirements and registration fees compared to sole proprietorships.
- **Registration**: To establish an LLC, you must register with the **Supreme Court's Registry Office** and obtain a business registration certificate from the tax office. Documentation such as your Articles of Incorporation and information on shareholders is required.

Corporation (Chusik Hoesa)

A **Chusik Hoesa** (Corporation) is ideal for larger businesses or those planning to operate on a large scale in South Korea. This structure allows for issuing shares and raising substantial capital but comes with stricter regulatory requirements.

- **Advantages**: Access to greater capital through shares, limited liability, and strong credibility.
- **Disadvantages**: Complex setup process, strict regulatory requirements, and higher costs.
- **Registration**: Corporations must register with the Supreme Court's Registry Office and apply for a business registration certificate. A Chusik Hoesa also requires the appointment of at least one director and must hold annual general meetings.

Branch Office or Liaison Office

Foreign businesses looking to enter the South Korean market can also set up a **branch office** or **liaison office**. A branch office can engage in commercial activities, while a liaison office is limited to market research and cannot engage in sales.

- **Branch Office**: Suitable if you plan to conduct business transactions directly within South Korea. It requires registration with the Supreme Court's Registry Office and the Financial Supervisory Service (FSS).

- **Liaison Office**: Ideal for market research or supporting an overseas business. It does not require registration with the Supreme Court but must be registered with the FSS.

3.2 Managing Taxes and VAT

Understanding the South Korean tax system is essential to ensure compliance and avoid penalties. South Korea's tax regime includes corporate tax, VAT, and income tax, all managed by the **National Tax Service (NTS)**.

Corporate Tax

Corporate tax is levied on all businesses operating in South Korea. The rate varies depending on the annual income of the business.

- **Rates (as of 2024)**:
    - **10%** on income up to KRW 200 million
    - **20%** on income between KRW 200 million and KRW 20 billion
    - **22%** on income above KRW 20 billion

Corporate tax returns must be filed annually, and businesses are encouraged to keep clear records of all transactions for accurate tax reporting.

Value-Added Tax (VAT)

Value-Added Tax (VAT) applies to most goods and services in South Korea, with the standard rate set at **10%**.

- **Registration**: Businesses with annual sales above KRW 30 million must register for VAT. Registration is done through the local District Tax Office.
- **VAT Returns**: VAT returns are submitted quarterly, and businesses are required to maintain detailed records of all transactions. Failure to file or late filing can lead to penalties.

Income Tax (for Sole Proprietors)

If you operate as a sole proprietor, you will pay **income tax** on your business profits rather than corporate tax.

- **Tax Rates**:
  - Rates range from 6% to 42%, depending on income.
  - Income tax must be filed annually, and you may be eligible for certain deductions.

Withholding Tax

Withholding tax applies to payments made to foreign entities or individuals. If you are receiving payment from a South Korean entity, they may withhold tax on the payment, typically at a rate of **15.4%**.

3.3 Understanding South Korean Consumer Protection Laws

South Korea has strict consumer protection laws to ensure that buyers receive fair treatment and high-quality products. Compliance with these laws is essential, especially if you sell directly to consumers (B2C).

Right to Return and Refunds

South Korean consumers have the right to return or exchange most goods within seven days if purchased online or over the phone. This "cooling-off period" is mandatory for remote transactions, and businesses must provide a full refund, including delivery costs.

- **Exceptions**: Exceptions may apply to items like perishables or personalised goods. Clearly outline any specific return policies on your website or sales materials.

Product Safety Standards

South Korea enforces strict safety standards for products, particularly electronics, cosmetics, and food items. Products must meet these safety requirements before they are sold, including required certifications or testing.

- **KC Mark**: Many products in South Korea require the **KC (Korea Certification) mark**, which certifies that the product meets safety, health, and environmental standards. Electronics, toys, and certain household goods fall under this requirement.

Data Protection (PIPA)

South Korea's **Personal Information Protection Act (PIPA)** governs how businesses collect, store, and use customer data. Compliance with PIPA is mandatory, particularly for e-commerce businesses or those using customer data for marketing.

- **Privacy Policies**: Clearly state how you handle personal information in a privacy policy on your website or sales materials. Customers must be informed of how their data will be used and have the right to request the deletion of their information.

Advertising and Labelling Laws

South Korea has stringent advertising and labelling laws to ensure transparency and honesty in marketing.

- **Labelling**: Products must be clearly labelled with information such as ingredients (for food and cosmetics), allergens, and usage instructions.
- **Misleading Advertising**: False claims about product benefits or performance are strictly regulated. Ensure that all advertising is truthful and does not exaggerate

the benefits of your products.

Chapter 3 - Summary

Setting up a business in South Korea requires careful consideration of the appropriate business structure, compliance with tax obligations, and adherence to consumer protection laws. Whether you choose a sole proprietorship, LLC, or corporation, understanding the legal requirements and tax system will help you operate smoothly and avoid regulatory issues. As a market that values quality, transparency, and consumer rights, South Korea rewards businesses that take compliance seriously and operate with integrity.

CHAPTER 4: WHAT TO SELL IN SOUTH KOREA: MARKET INSIGHTS

South Korea is a trend-sensitive and highly competitive market where consumer preferences shift quickly, often influenced by pop culture, technology, and global trends. Understanding what products resonate with South Korean consumers, and tailoring your offerings to meet these tastes, is essential for success. In this chapter, we'll explore some of the best-selling product categories, identify key trends shaping the South Korean market, and highlight seasonal and regional variations in consumer demand.

4.1 Best-Selling Product Categories

South Korean consumers are discerning and place a high value on quality, innovation, and design. Below are some of the top product categories that perform well in the South Korean market.

Beauty and Skincare

South Korea is globally recognised for its pioneering skincare and beauty products, often referred to as **K-beauty**. With a strong focus on skincare, South Korean consumers are particularly interested in products that enhance skin health, prevent ageing, and offer unique, effective formulations.

- **What Sells**: Skincare items such as cleansers, serums, masks, and moisturisers are popular, especially those with natural, high-quality ingredients. Products that incorporate Korean skincare methods, such as sheet masks and essences, continue to perform well.

- **Trends**: Products with eco-friendly packaging, cruelty-free labels, and natural ingredients are gaining popularity as South Korean consumers become more environmentally conscious.

Fashion and Apparel

South Korean consumers are style-conscious and quick to adopt global fashion trends. The fashion market is diverse, covering everything from luxury brands to affordable streetwear, with a strong preference for unique and fashionable designs.

- **What Sells**: Streetwear, minimalist fashion, and trendy accessories like handbags, hats, and jewellery are popular, especially among younger consumers. Korean consumers also have a keen interest in foreign brands and luxury items.

- **Trends**: Fashion trends change rapidly in South Korea, often influenced by K-pop idols, K-dramas, and social media. Brands that can keep up with these fast-moving trends are more likely to succeed.

Technology and Gadgets

South Korean consumers are highly tech-savvy and enthusiastic about the latest technology. The demand for gadgets and electronics is strong, particularly for products that offer convenience, entertainment, or health benefits.

- **What Sells**: Smartphones, wearables (e.g., smartwatches, fitness trackers), wireless earphones, and gaming accessories are popular. Home automation devices, such as smart speakers and home security systems, are also seeing growth.

- **Trends**: Products with unique features or cutting-edge technology, such as AI integration or IoT compatibility, tend to attract South Korean consumers, who value innovation and convenience.

Gourmet Food and Beverages

South Korean consumers are increasingly interested in gourmet foods, health-conscious options, and unique beverages. With the rise of social media, visually appealing foods that offer an Instagram-worthy experience are particularly popular.

- **What Sells**: Artisanal snacks, premium teas and coffees, organic and vegan foods, and international delicacies have strong appeal. Health-conscious foods, including gluten-free and low-sugar options, are gaining popularity as consumers become more aware of health and wellness.

- **Trends**: Food delivery apps are very popular in South Korea, and products that cater to the delivery market—such as ready-to-eat meals or snack boxes—have strong potential.

Home and Lifestyle Products

The home décor and lifestyle market is growing as more South Koreans focus on enhancing their living spaces. This trend is driven by the popularity of interior design content on social media and a desire for comfortable, aesthetically pleasing environments.

- **What Sells**: Home décor items, furniture, storage solutions, and kitchenware are popular. Consumers are also interested in products that promote relaxation and wellbeing, such as scented candles, diffusers, and home spa items.

- **Trends**: Minimalist, eco-friendly, and space-saving products are favoured, especially among urban consumers living in smaller apartments.

4.2 Seasonal and Regional Trends

Understanding South Korea's seasonal and regional trends can help you tailor your product offerings to meet changing consumer demands. South Korean consumers are highly responsive to seasonal products and events, and certain times of year present unique opportunities for specific types of goods.

Seasonal Trends

- **Lunar New Year (Seollal):** This is one of the biggest holidays in South Korea, usually celebrated in January or February. Consumers purchase gifts for family members, such as high-quality food items, skincare products, and health supplements. Traditional clothing (hanbok) and home décor items are also popular during this period.

- **Chuseok (Harvest Festival):** Similar to Thanksgiving, Chuseok is celebrated in September or October and is a time for families to come together. Gift-giving is customary, with a preference for food hampers, premium fruits, meat, and health products.

- **Christmas and Year-End:** Although Christmas is not a traditional holiday in South Korea, it has become a popular time for gift-giving, especially among younger consumers and couples. Festive items, winter fashion, and luxury goods often see a surge in demand during this season.

- **Summer Festival Season:** Summer is festival season in South Korea, with events across the country. Products such as fashion accessories, sunscreen, portable fans, and picnic-related items tend to perform well during this time.

Regional Trends

- **Seoul:** As the capital and largest city, Seoul has a diverse and fast-paced consumer base. Consumers in Seoul are particularly responsive to global trends, and products that showcase innovation and high quality are popular. The city's tech-savvy population makes it an ideal market for electronics, fashion, and luxury goods.

- **Busan:** Busan, known for its port and beaches, has a strong market for seafood, local delicacies, and tourism-related products. Lifestyle and wellness products, particularly those suited for outdoor activities, are also popular due to the city's coastal culture.

- **Jeju Island**: Jeju is a tourist hotspot known for its natural beauty, eco-tourism, and unique local products, such as Jeju tea and volcanic skincare products. Visitors to Jeju often look for souvenirs, eco-friendly goods, and wellness products that reflect the island's culture and environment.

4.3 Sustainability and Ethical Products

Sustainability is increasingly important to South Korean consumers, especially younger buyers. A growing awareness of environmental issues, driven by global movements and social media, has created demand for products that are eco-friendly, ethically sourced, and socially responsible.

Eco-Friendly Products

Products with sustainable packaging, reusable materials, or reduced environmental impact resonate strongly with South Korean consumers. Eco-friendly products are particularly popular in sectors like beauty, fashion, and home goods.

- **What Sells**: Reusable water bottles, bamboo toothbrushes, zero-waste beauty products, and biodegradable packaging are all attractive options. Minimalist packaging, which reduces waste and aligns with South Korean aesthetic preferences, is also well-received.

Ethically Sourced Goods

South Korean consumers are becoming more conscious of how their purchases impact the environment and communities. Products that are fair-trade certified or ethically sourced tend to appeal to those who value corporate responsibility.

- **What Sells**: Fair-trade food products (e.g., coffee, chocolate, tea), clothing made from organic or recycled materials, and items that support social or environmental causes. Transparent labelling that informs consumers about ethical practices adds value and trust to these products.

Local and Artisanal Products

There is a growing appreciation for locally made and artisanal products, which are seen as authentic and often have a story behind them. This is particularly true for crafts, fashion, and food, where consumers enjoy unique items that are not mass-produced.

- **What Sells**: Handmade crafts, traditional Korean items, local foods, and products with a focus on craftsmanship. Artisanal goods that showcase cultural heritage and quality are well-received, especially by tourists and consumers seeking something distinct.

Chapter 4 - Summary

South Korea's fast-paced and trend-driven consumer market offers numerous opportunities across various product categories. From high-quality skincare and fashion to tech gadgets and gourmet food, South Korean consumers appreciate products that align with their interests in quality, innovation, and sustainability. Understanding regional and seasonal trends, along with the growing demand for eco-friendly and ethical products, can help you tailor your offerings to the South Korean market and maximise your success.

CHAPTER 5: SELLING INDUSTRIAL PRODUCTS AND SERVICES IN SOUTH KOREA

South Korea's industrial sector is highly developed, driven by industries such as automotive, electronics, shipbuilding, and machinery. With a strong focus on technology, innovation, and quality, South Korea has become one of the world's leading industrial economies. Selling industrial products and services in South Korea requires an understanding of the local market demands, business culture, and regulatory requirements. This chapter provides insights into the South Korean industrial sector, the best approaches to market entry, and strategies for building partnerships with local businesses.

5.1 Understanding the South Korean Industrial Market

South Korea's industrial market is diverse and rapidly evolving, with an emphasis on advanced manufacturing, automation, and sustainable practices. The country has a large demand for industrial products that enhance productivity, quality, and technological innovation.

Key Sectors for Industrial Products

- Automotive: South Korea is home to major automotive manufacturers like Hyundai and Kia, and there is a continuous demand for advanced machinery, robotics, and automotive components that enhance manufacturing efficiency and quality.

- Electronics and Semiconductors: South Korea is one of the world's largest producers of electronics and semiconductors. The market has high demand for precision equipment, cleanroom technologies, and advanced manufacturing tools.

- Shipbuilding and Marine: South Korea is a global leader in shipbuilding, with a focus on sustainability and eco-friendly technologies. There is strong demand for industrial products such as specialised machinery, marine engines, and green technologies.

- Machinery and Robotics: As automation becomes increasingly important, South Korea's demand for industrial robotics, AI-driven manufacturing solutions, and high-tech machinery is on the rise, especially for precision manufacturing and assembly.

Focus on Quality and Innovation

South Korean industries prioritise quality, innovation, and durability. South Korean buyers expect industrial products and services that meet high standards and can demonstrate a tangible impact on efficiency and output.

- Quality Assurance: Products must comply with stringent quality standards. Any certifications, such as ISO or CE, can enhance credibility.

- Innovation: South Korean companies are forward-looking and value cutting-edge solutions. Products that incorporate the latest technologies, such as IoT integration or AI-driven functions, are well-regarded.

- Sustainability: With a growing focus on sustainable practices, South Korean industries increasingly seek eco-friendly industrial solutions. Sustainable machinery, energy-efficient equipment, and environmentally responsible practices are highly valued.

5.2 Market Entry Strategies for Industrial Products and Services

Entering the South Korean industrial market requires a strategic approach. Building credibility, partnering with local companies, and tailoring your offerings to meet local demands are essential steps.

Establishing Local Partnerships

Local partnerships are a valuable asset in South Korea's industrial sector. Collaborating with South Korean distributors, agents, or manufacturers can help you navigate local regulations, access networks, and gain insights into the market.

- Choosing the Right Partner: Seek partners who have experience in your industry, a solid reputation, and established networks. Distributors or agents with a technical background in your field can provide crucial support and insights.

- Joint Ventures and Strategic Alliances: Forming a joint venture with a South Korean company can help you access local expertise, resources, and connections. This approach is particularly beneficial for businesses with limited experience in the South Korean market.

Localising Marketing and Technical Documentation

Localising your marketing materials, technical documentation, and support resources is essential to connect with South Korean industrial buyers. They appreciate detailed, accurate, and well-presented information in Korean.

- Technical Documentation: Translate manuals, technical specifications, and safety information into Korean. Clear and precise documentation can help ensure compliance with local safety standards and foster trust.

- Website Localisation: Develop a Korean-language website or a dedicated Korean section on your existing site. South Korean companies are likely to research your products online, so an optimised, localised website will enhance your credibility.

Attending Industry Events and Trade Shows

Trade shows and industry events provide excellent opportunities to showcase your products, meet potential clients, and establish a presence in the South Korean market. Key events such as the Seoul International Manufacturing Technology Show (SIMTOS) and Korea Industrial Machinery Expo draw industrial professionals from across the country.

- Networking: Use trade shows to build relationships with potential customers, distributors, and suppliers. Networking at these events is often the first step to securing long-term partnerships.

- Product Demonstrations: Demonstrating your product's functionality and benefits at industry events can be highly effective, particularly in a market that values technical detail and innovation.

5.3 Compliance and Regulatory Considerations

South Korea has strict regulations governing the quality, safety, and environmental impact of industrial products. Familiarising yourself with the regulatory environment is essential to ensure your products meet local standards and avoid compliance issues.

Product Safety Standards and Certifications

South Korea requires many industrial products to meet safety standards, often requiring third-party certifications.

- KC Certification: The Korea Certification (KC) mark is mandatory for many industrial products sold in South Korea, including machinery and electrical equipment. It certifies compliance with local safety and quality standards.

- Other Certifications: Depending on the industry, other certifications such as ISO (International Organisation for Standardisation) may be required or recommended. South Korean buyers often look for these certifications as indicators of quality and reliability.

Import Regulations and Tariffs

Understanding import regulations, tariffs, and duty requirements is essential when entering the South Korean market.

- Customs and Documentation: Ensure that all necessary import documents are in order, including invoices, certificates of origin, and product specifications. South Korea has strict customs regulations, and documentation errors can result in delays.

- Duty-Free and Reduced Tariff Opportunities: The Korea-United Kingdom Free Trade Agreement offers opportunities for reduced or duty-free import on certain products. Check if your products qualify for preferential tariffs under this agreement.

Environmental Regulations

South Korea is becoming increasingly focused on sustainability, and environmental regulations are tightening. Many South Korean companies expect suppliers to adhere to eco-friendly practices and may request information on the environmental impact of your products.

- Eco-Friendly Certifications: Products that hold eco-friendly certifications, such as ISO 14001 for environmental management, can have a competitive edge.

- Waste Management and Recycling Requirements: Some industries, such as electronics and automotive, have regulations requiring recycling or waste management plans for certain products. Ensure your products comply with local waste disposal and recycling laws.

5.4 Building Relationships and Sales Channels

Building a strong network and understanding South Korean business practices are crucial for establishing a successful sales channel for industrial products. South Korean businesses value trust and long-term partnerships, so investing in relationship-building is essential.

Establishing Trust and Credibility

Credibility is critical when selling industrial products in South Korea, as buyers seek reliable suppliers who can consistently deliver high-quality products.

- Quality Assurance: Providing a warranty, after-sales service, or a quality guarantee can enhance trust. South Korean companies value suppliers who can demonstrate a commitment to product support and maintenance.

- Customer Testimonials and Case Studies: Sharing case studies, testimonials, and references from well-known clients can build your credibility. South Korean buyers are more likely to trust products that have proven performance with other reputable companies.

Developing a Dedicated Sales Team or Local Office

A dedicated sales team or local office can help manage client relationships, oversee sales activities, and provide technical support. Having a local presence is especially beneficial in a market where in-person interactions and quick responses to customer inquiries are valued.

- Sales Engineers and Technical Support: Employing sales engineers or technical support staff who can understand and explain your product's technical specifications will be beneficial. South Korean buyers often prefer to interact with knowledgeable representatives who can answer specific, technical questions.

- Local Office Benefits: Establishing a local office shows commitment to the South Korean market and improves your ability to respond quickly to customer needs. It also makes it easier to manage logistics, compliance, and after-sales service.

Offering After-Sales Support and Maintenance

Providing after-sales support and maintenance is essential for building a loyal client base in South Korea's industrial market. South Korean companies prefer suppliers who offer long-term support, reliable maintenance options, and swift issue resolution.

- Training and Maintenance Packages: Offering training for client staff on equipment use and maintenance can set you apart from competitors. Maintenance packages or service contracts are also valued, as they ensure clients have dependable, long-term support.

- Spare Parts and Repair Services: The availability of spare parts and repair services can be a deciding factor for South Korean companies. Establishing a local spare parts inventory or repair centre can improve customer satisfaction and enhance your reputation for reliability.

Chapter 5 - Summary

Selling industrial products and services in South Korea's competitive and advanced market requires a deep understanding of local industry demands, regulatory compliance, and a commitment to quality and innovation. By establishing local partnerships, attending industry events, and meeting regulatory requirements, you can successfully navigate the South Korean market. Building trust through quality assurance, after-sales support, and tailored marketing efforts will help you create long-term relationships with South Korean companies, unlocking significant opportunities for growth in this industrial powerhouse.

CHAPTER 6: SELLING AT MARKETS AND FAIRS IN SOUTH KOREA

South Korea has a rich culture of markets and fairs, where everything from traditional crafts and gourmet foods to trendy fashion items is sold. Selling at these venues can provide an excellent opportunity to reach both local consumers and tourists, allowing you to engage directly with customers, build brand awareness, and gain valuable feedback on your products. In this chapter, we'll explore the famous markets in South Korea, guide you on setting up an appealing stall, and provide tips for connecting with customers effectively.

6.1 Famous Markets in South Korea

South Korea's markets range from large, bustling street markets in Seoul to local, traditional markets in smaller cities. Each market has its unique atmosphere and draws a different type of consumer, making it important to choose the right location for your products.

Dongdaemun Market (Seoul)

- **Overview**: Located in Seoul, Dongdaemun is one of South Korea's largest and most famous shopping districts, particularly known for its fashion wholesale markets. Open day and night, Dongdaemun attracts both locals and tourists looking for clothing, accessories, and fabrics.

- **What Sells**: Fashion, textiles, and trendy accessories are popular items. If you're selling clothing or unique fashion pieces, this market provides a prime opportunity to reach fashion-forward shoppers.

Namdaemun Market (Seoul)

- **Overview**: As South Korea's oldest market, Namdaemun offers a variety of goods, from clothing and accessories to local food and souvenirs. The market is highly popular with both locals and tourists and has a lively atmosphere with hundreds of stalls.

- **What Sells**: Local foods, handicrafts, souvenirs, and household items are popular. This is an excellent venue for selling traditional crafts or unique items with cultural significance.

Gukje Market (Busan)

- **Overview**: Gukje Market, located in Busan, is one of South Korea's largest traditional markets. Known for its variety of products, from clothing to electronics, the market has a rich history and draws a diverse crowd of both locals and visitors.

- **What Sells**: Local delicacies, handmade goods, clothing, and electronics. Gukje Market is ideal for sellers offering diverse or culturally inspired items that reflect the local vibe.

Insadong (Seoul)

- **Overview**: Insadong is one of Seoul's cultural hubs, filled with art galleries, tea houses, and shops selling traditional Korean crafts. The area is popular with tourists and locals interested in South Korea's cultural heritage.

- **What Sells**: Art, pottery, calligraphy, traditional clothing, and souvenirs. If you're selling artisanal crafts or products with a cultural story, Insadong is the ideal market.

Jeju Five-Day Market (Jeju Island)

- **Overview**: Held every five days, this market on Jeju Island showcases local produce, seafood, and handmade goods. It is a traditional market with a local charm, popular among residents and visitors seeking authentic Jeju products.

- **What Sells**: Fresh produce, seafood, traditional foods, and handicrafts. This market is great for selling items that reflect Jeju's unique local culture or artisanal foods.

6.2 Setting Up Your Stall

A well-organised and visually appealing stall is crucial for attracting customers at South Korean markets and fairs. With so many options to choose from, customers are more likely to visit stalls that look professional, welcoming, and engaging.

Stall Design and Layout

- **Create an Open Layout**: Arrange your products to make them easy to browse. Avoid clutter, as crowded displays can deter customers. Keep your most popular or eye-catching products at the front to attract attention.

- **Use Height and Layers**: Use shelving or raised displays to create different levels for your products, adding visual interest and making it easier for customers to see everything. Small risers, stands, or crates can give your stall a professional look without needing too much setup.

- **Branding and Signage**: Display clear signage with your brand name and logo to make your stall recognisable. Signs indicating any special offers or the story behind your products can also enhance the customer experience.

Lighting and Décor

- **Portable Lighting**: If you're selling at a night market or an indoor fair, portable LED lights can make your stall stand out. Soft, warm lighting often works well to create a welcoming atmosphere.

- **Cultural Touches**: Adding small decorations that tie in with your brand or products can enhance your stall's visual appeal. For example, if you're selling eco-friendly goods, adding natural elements like plants can reinforce your brand image.

Packaging and Presentation

- **Professional Packaging**: South Korean consumers appreciate well-packaged products. Invest in quality, eco-friendly packaging that reflects your brand values and offers a pleasant unboxing experience.
- **Gift Wrapping**: Many South Koreans buy market items as gifts. Offering free or paid gift-wrapping services can be a great way to add value, especially during festive seasons like Chuseok or Christmas.

6.3 Connecting with Customers

Engaging directly with customers is one of the best advantages of selling at markets and fairs. South Korean consumers respond well to friendly, knowledgeable vendors who are passionate about their products.

Polite and Friendly Interaction

- **Greet Customers Warmly**: A simple greeting, such as "Annyeonghaseyo" (hello), is polite and welcoming. Being approachable and ready to answer questions can go a long way in making a positive impression.
- **Avoid Hard Selling**: South Korean customers appreciate a low-pressure shopping experience. Instead of pushing for sales, provide information on the product and allow customers to browse at their own pace.

Telling Your Product's Story

- **Share the Story Behind Your Products**: South Korean consumers appreciate products with a story, whether it's the inspiration behind a design, the craftsmanship involved, or the environmental impact. Explain why your product is unique and the value it offers.

- **Use Bilingual Materials**: If possible, provide bilingual signage or brochures that share information about your products in both Korean and English. This is especially useful for attracting tourists and local consumers who may prefer English descriptions.

Encouraging Sales and Repeat Business

- **Discounts and Bundle Deals**: Offering discounts for purchasing multiple items, such as "buy one, get one half-price," can encourage customers to buy more. Bundle deals are also popular, especially for complementary products.

- **Loyalty Incentives**: Consider offering loyalty incentives for repeat customers, like a stamp card or small gifts after a certain number of purchases. This helps to build customer loyalty and may lead to more repeat business.

- **Promotional Materials**: Providing business cards, flyers, or brochures with information about your social media or website can help customers follow up with you after their visit. This is especially important if you plan to attend other markets or have an online store they can visit later.

6.4 Navigating Market Regulations and Costs

Before setting up at a market or fair, it's important to familiarise yourself with the regulations, costs, and requirements for vendors. These can vary by location and market type, so it's always best to check with market organisers in advance.

Applying for a Stall

- **Application Process**: Most markets require vendors to apply for a stall in advance. Applications are often reviewed to ensure that the products are suitable for the market's theme or standards. Check the market's website or contact organisers for information on the application process and deadlines.

- **Required Permits**: Some markets, especially larger ones, may require vendors to have certain permits or certificates. For example, if you're selling food products, you may need health and safety certification from the **Korea Food and Drug Administration (KFDA)**.

Stall Fees

- **Cost of Renting a Stall**: Stall fees vary greatly depending on the market's location, popularity, and the size of your stall. Popular markets in Seoul, like Dongdaemun or Insadong, tend to have higher fees, while smaller markets or community fairs may charge lower rates.

- **Revenue Sharing**: Some markets charge a percentage of your revenue instead of a flat fee. Be sure to clarify the cost structure with organisers to avoid surprises.

Insurance and Liability

- **Public Liability Insurance**: Some markets may require vendors to have public liability insurance, covering potential accidents or damage related to your stall. While not always mandatory, it can be a good idea to protect yourself and your business.

- **Product Liability**: If you're selling consumable products like food or skincare, product liability insurance is recommended to protect you against claims related to product safety or health concerns.

Chapter 6 - Summary

Selling at markets and fairs in South Korea provides a valuable opportunity to reach a wide range of customers, from locals to international visitors. By setting up an attractive stall, engaging politely with customers, and offering value-added services like packaging and loyalty incentives, you can build strong relationships and increase your sales. Familiarising yourself with market regulations, fees, and requirements will help ensure a smooth and successful experience at South Korea's bustling and vibrant markets.

CHAPTER 7: SELLING ONLINE IN SOUTH KOREA

South Korea is one of the world's most connected and tech-savvy countries, making it an ideal market for e-commerce. With a high level of internet penetration and a digitally engaged population, South Korean consumers expect seamless online shopping experiences, rapid delivery, and a wide array of payment options. In this chapter, we'll cover the essentials for establishing an online presence, choosing the right e-commerce platforms, and crafting a digital marketing strategy tailored to South Korean consumers.

7.1 Popular E-Commerce Platforms in South Korea

Choosing the right e-commerce platform is essential for reaching South Korean consumers effectively. South Korea has a range of popular online marketplaces, each catering to different types of products and audiences.

Coupang

Often referred to as the "Amazon of South Korea," **Coupang** is the largest online retailer in the country. Known for its **Rocket Delivery** service, which offers next-day or even same-day delivery, Coupang is popular for its convenience and extensive product range.

- **Advantages**: Large customer base, trusted brand, and advanced logistics network. Coupang's efficient delivery system can boost sales for products where fast delivery is a key factor.

- **Best For**: Consumer goods, electronics, household items, and products where convenience and rapid delivery are important.

11st Street (11　　　　　　　　　　　　　)

11st Street is one of South Korea's top online marketplaces, offering a wide range of products from fashion and beauty to electronics and home goods. With its extensive selection, 11st Street attracts a diverse audience and provides a user-friendly shopping experience.

- **Advantages**: Large user base, well-established platform, and marketing support options for sellers.
- **Best For**: Fashion, beauty, lifestyle products, and tech gadgets.

Gmarket

Gmarket is a major e-commerce platform that caters to both South Korean and international shoppers. It's known for offering a broad selection of products and often features deals and discounts that attract price-sensitive consumers.

- **Advantages**: Large selection of products, international reach, and integration with popular South Korean payment options.
- **Best For**: Fashion, electronics, household goods, and products that appeal to value-conscious consumers.

Naver Smart Store

Naver, South Korea's leading search engine, also operates **Naver Smart Store**, which integrates directly with Naver's search results. Smart Store allows businesses to create a branded online shop and leverage Naver's SEO capabilities, which can significantly improve visibility.

- **Advantages**: Integration with Naver's ecosystem, strong SEO support, and visibility among local consumers.
- **Best For**: Small businesses, niche brands, and products that benefit from enhanced online visibility.

Café24

Café24 is a popular platform for businesses looking to set up their own e-commerce websites. Café24 offers customisable website templates, integrated payment options, and a range of tools to support local and international sales.

- **Advantages**: Full control over branding, customisable website options, and multi-language support.
- **Best For**: Businesses looking to establish a unique online presence and brands targeting international consumers.

7.2 Crafting a Localised Marketing Strategy

Marketing to South Korean consumers requires a localised approach that considers their preferences, behaviours, and online habits. From website localisation to digital advertising, tailoring your marketing strategy will help you stand out in a competitive online market.

Website Localisation and SEO

Localising your website is crucial for engaging South Korean consumers. This includes using Korean language, local payment options, and optimising for local search engines.

- **Korean Language**: Ensure that your website or online store is available in Korean. Consumers are more likely to engage with brands that communicate in their native language.
- **SEO on Naver**: Unlike most countries, South Korea's dominant search engine is not Google but **Naver**. Naver has its own SEO practices, and optimising your site for Naver can improve your visibility. Focus on keywords relevant to your product and industry, and consider setting up a **Naver Blog** or participating in **Naver KnowledgeIn** to increase brand visibility.
- **Mobile Optimisation**: South Korean consumers are highly mobile-focused, so ensure your site is optimised for mobile shopping, including fast load times, responsive design, and easy-to-use navigation.

Social Media Marketing

Social media is a powerful tool in South Korea, where platforms like **Instagram**, **YouTube**, and **KakaoTalk** are widely used for product discovery, brand engagement, and customer service.

- **Instagram**: South Korean consumers, especially younger demographics, rely heavily on Instagram for trend discovery. Post visually appealing content, use hashtags, and consider setting up an Instagram Shop for easy shopping.

- **YouTube**: YouTube is a popular platform for reviews, tutorials, and product showcases. Collaborating with YouTube influencers or creating your own branded channel can help attract a dedicated audience.

- **KakaoTalk**: **KakaoTalk**, South Korea's leading messaging app, offers business tools such as **KakaoTalk Channels**, which allow brands to engage directly with customers, provide updates, and send promotions. KakaoTalk is highly integrated into South Korean daily life and is an effective way to maintain a connection with your audience.

Email Marketing

Although email marketing is less prevalent in South Korea than in other countries, it can still be effective, especially when combined with mobile alerts. Regular newsletters, exclusive offers, and personalised recommendations can help drive repeat sales and build customer loyalty.

- **Personalisation**: Personalised recommendations based on browsing history or past purchases resonate well with South Korean consumers. Use data to tailor emails to customer preferences.

- **Seasonal Campaigns**: Create email campaigns around key shopping periods such as Lunar New Year, Chuseok, and other major holidays. Highlight any special promotions or limited-time offers.

7.3 Payment Methods and Secure Transactions

Offering secure, convenient payment options is essential for success in South Korea's e-commerce market. South Korean consumers expect a range of local payment options, and trust is paramount when it comes to handling financial transactions.

Popular Payment Methods in South Korea

- **Credit and Debit Cards**: Most South Koreans use credit or debit cards for online purchases. Visa, Mastercard, and local cards like **Shinhan** and **KB Kookmin Card** are widely accepted.

- **KakaoPay and Naver Pay**: Mobile payment solutions such as **KakaoPay** and **Naver Pay** are highly popular, especially among younger consumers. These options allow users to pay securely without entering card details, providing a quick and convenient experience.

- **Payco**: **Payco** is another mobile payment platform commonly used for online shopping and in-app purchases. It's integrated with various e-commerce sites, making it a convenient choice for local consumers.

Secure Transactions and Trust Signals

South Korean consumers value security and privacy when shopping online. Building trust by offering secure payment methods and showcasing trust signals can help boost your credibility.

- **SSL Certificates**: Ensure that your website is secured with an **SSL certificate** (indicated by the padlock symbol in the browser's address bar) to encrypt data and protect customer information during transactions.

- **Trust Badges**: Display trust badges, such as **KCP** or **INICIS** (South Korean payment gateways), to reassure customers of your website's security.

- **Customer Reviews**: South Korean consumers frequently

read reviews before making a purchase. Incorporate customer reviews, testimonials, or ratings on your product pages to build trust.

7.4 Shipping and Logistics for South Korean Consumers

Shipping speed and reliability are key considerations for South Korean online shoppers. Many consumers expect next-day or even same-day delivery, particularly in major urban areas.

Domestic Shipping Solutions

- **Korea Post**: **Korea Post** provides reliable and affordable shipping options for domestic deliveries. It's a good choice for smaller parcels or regular business shipping needs.

- **Private Couriers**: Companies like **CJ Logistics**, **Hanjin Express**, and **Lotte Global Logistics** offer fast, reliable shipping services across South Korea, with options for express and same-day delivery. These couriers are popular among e-commerce businesses due to their efficiency and widespread network.

Free and Fast Delivery Expectations

Many South Korean consumers are accustomed to quick and often free delivery. While it may not always be feasible to offer same-day delivery, providing express options and offering free shipping for orders above a certain amount can help you stay competitive.

- **Click-and-Collect**: South Korean consumers appreciate click-and-collect options, where they can pick up their items at nearby convenience stores or designated lockers. This option is popular as it adds convenience, especially for urban consumers.

Returns and Customer Service

- **Flexible Return Policies**: South Korean consumers

expect flexible return policies. Offering free or hassle-free returns within 7 to 14 days can help build customer trust and encourage purchases.

- **Clear Communication**: Ensure that your shipping and returns policies are clearly stated on your website, including information on delivery times, return procedures, and any associated fees.

7.5 Managing Customer Service for E-Commerce

Providing exceptional customer service is essential for building trust and loyalty in the online marketplace. In South Korea, consumers expect responsive and helpful service, especially when it comes to handling queries or addressing concerns.

Customer Support Channels

- **Live Chat**: Many online shoppers prefer live chat for quick responses. Implementing a live chat feature on your website or using KakaoTalk for customer support can enhance customer satisfaction.

- **Email and Phone Support**: Offering both email and phone support gives customers flexibility in how they reach out. Be prompt in responding to emails (ideally within 24 hours), and ensure phone support is available during business hours in the South Korean time zone.

Handling Complaints and Feedback

- **Timely Responses**: South Korean consumers value timely responses. If a customer raises an issue, responding quickly with a clear resolution—such as a refund or exchange—can help prevent negative reviews and build loyalty.

- **Encourage Reviews**: Positive reviews significantly boost your credibility. Encourage satisfied customers to leave reviews on your website or platforms like Naver or Kakao. Responding to feedback, both positive and negative, shows you value customer satisfaction.

Chapter 7 - Summary

Selling online in South Korea offers vast opportunities, but success requires careful attention to detail in your e-commerce setup, marketing strategy, and customer service. By choosing the right platform, localising your marketing efforts, offering secure payment options, and prioritising quick, reliable shipping, you can build a thriving online business that resonates with South Korean consumers. With a market that values convenience, trust, and high standards, ensuring your online presence meets these expectations is crucial for long-term success.

CHAPTER 8: MARKETING STRATEGIES FOR SOUTH KOREAN CONSUMERS

Marketing in South Korea requires a blend of digital engagement, localised content, and trend awareness. South Korean consumers are highly engaged with social media, responsive to influencer marketing, and quick to embrace the latest trends. Understanding the right channels, messages, and timing for your marketing efforts is essential for capturing attention and building loyalty in this competitive market.

In this chapter, we'll explore the most effective marketing strategies for reaching South Korean consumers, from social media engagement and search engine optimisation to influencer partnerships and seasonal campaigns.

8.1 Understanding South Korean Buyer Behaviour

South Korean consumers are some of the most tech-savvy and trend-sensitive in the world. They expect high quality and appreciate convenience, innovation, and strong brand identities. Understanding these core aspects of South Korean buyer behaviour will help you create a marketing strategy that resonates with this unique audience.

Trend Sensitivity

South Korean consumers are highly responsive to trends, often influenced by pop culture, social media, and global fashion movements. Trends can move quickly, especially in industries like fashion, beauty, and technology.

- **Quick Adaptation**: Keep up with the latest trends by monitoring South Korean influencers, K-pop culture, and popular brands. Being agile and responsive can help you adapt your product offerings and marketing messages to meet consumer expectations.

Digital Engagement and Mobile Usage

With one of the highest smartphone penetration rates globally, South Korean consumers are heavily mobile-focused. They shop, research products, and engage with brands primarily through their smartphones.

- **Mobile-First Approach**: Ensure all digital content is optimised for mobile devices. Responsive design, fast-loading pages, and mobile-friendly shopping experiences are essential.

- **Social Media and Messaging Apps**: Platforms like Instagram, KakaoTalk, and YouTube play a crucial role in brand engagement and product discovery.

Trust in Brand Reputation

Brand reputation is a key factor in South Korean consumer decisions. South Koreans often research brands and read reviews before purchasing, valuing reliability, quality, and customer service.

- **Build Credibility**: Highlight positive reviews, testimonials, and any certifications or awards your brand has received. Trust signals, such as customer endorsements and high ratings, are essential to establishing credibility.

8.2 Digital Marketing Channels

In South Korea, digital marketing is the most effective way to reach and engage consumers. A strategic presence across search engines, social media, and video platforms can help you connect with your target audience and boost brand visibility.

SEO on Naver and Google

South Korea's dominant search engine is **Naver**, rather than Google. To optimise your site for local search, it's essential to understand Naver's SEO practices and consider both Naver and Google for your SEO efforts.

- **Naver Blog and KnowledgeIn**: Engaging on Naver's blog and Q&A platform, **KnowledgeIn**, can help increase your brand's visibility. Answering relevant questions and sharing valuable content can establish your brand as an expert in your field.

- **Keyword Localisation**: Focus on keywords relevant to your product and industry, making sure to use Korean language keywords that resonate with your audience. Regularly updating your content with popular, seasonal, or trending keywords can help boost visibility.

Social Media Marketing

Social media is central to South Korean consumers' daily lives. Popular platforms include **Instagram**, **YouTube**, **KakaoTalk**, and increasingly, **TikTok**.

- **Instagram**: Visual content resonates strongly with South Korean consumers, and Instagram is a leading platform for product discovery. Use high-quality images, engaging captions, and hashtags to attract followers, and consider setting up an Instagram Shop for seamless in-app shopping.

- **YouTube**: Video content is extremely popular in South Korea. Product tutorials, reviews, and "unboxing" videos often drive significant engagement. Creating your own branded YouTube channel or partnering with influencers can help you reach a wide audience.

- **KakaoTalk Channels**: **KakaoTalk**, South Korea's top messaging app, allows businesses to create channels to share updates, promotions, and product information. This channel can be highly effective for building a loyal customer base and communicating directly with your audience.

Email Marketing

Email marketing, while not as prominent in South Korea as in other markets, can still be useful for customer engagement, particularly for exclusive offers and product launches.

- **Personalisation**: Personalised recommendations and offers are well-received. Use customer data to tailor email content to specific interests, browsing habits, or past purchases.

- **Combine with Mobile Alerts**: South Korean consumers are responsive to mobile notifications. Consider integrating email marketing with mobile alerts or KakaoTalk messages for greater engagement.

8.3 Influencer Marketing in South Korea

Influencer marketing is a powerful strategy in South Korea, especially in beauty, fashion, and lifestyle sectors. Influencers and celebrities have strong sway over consumer decisions, with K-pop idols and social media personalities playing significant roles in driving trends and brand popularity.

Choosing the Right Influencers

Choosing an influencer who aligns with your brand values and target audience is key. In South Korea, both **macro-influencers** (with larger followings) and **micro-influencers** (with smaller, highly engaged audiences) are effective, depending on your goals and budget.

- **K-Pop Idols and Celebrities**: Collaborations with K-pop stars or well-known actors are ideal for larger brands seeking mass visibility. However, these partnerships come with high costs.

- **YouTube and Instagram Influencers**: YouTube and Instagram influencers are effective for engaging niche audiences. **Beauty bloggers**, **fashion influencers**, and **tech reviewers** can help boost credibility and reach within specific demographics.

Influencer Campaigns

- **Product Reviews and Demonstrations**: Partner with influencers to create product reviews or demonstrations that highlight your product's benefits. Authentic, relatable content resonates well with South Korean audiences.

- **Sponsored Posts and Giveaways**: Sponsored posts, particularly those that feature influencer recommendations, can drive engagement. Running giveaways or "like and follow" competitions with influencers can increase your social media following and brand visibility.

8.4 Traditional Marketing Methods

While digital marketing dominates, traditional methods such as print advertising, outdoor advertising, and direct mail are still relevant, especially when targeting specific demographics or building brand awareness in certain regions.

Print Advertising

Print advertising in magazines and newspapers is particularly effective for reaching older audiences or professionals. Magazines covering lifestyle, fashion, and technology provide excellent platforms for reaching targeted demographics.

- **Best For**: Niche markets, luxury products, and targeting specific audiences. High-quality print ads in popular magazines can enhance brand prestige and credibility.

Outdoor Advertising

Billboards, bus stop ads, and posters are widely used in urban centres like Seoul and Busan, where they reach a large number of consumers. Outdoor advertising is especially effective for building brand awareness and promoting seasonal sales.

- **Best For**: Mass-market products, seasonal promotions, and building brand visibility. Outdoor ads work well in high-traffic locations, particularly near shopping districts or transit stations.

Direct Mail and Catalogues

Direct mail campaigns, including catalogues and brochures, can be useful for targeting specific consumer groups, particularly in suburban areas where digital reach may be lower.

- **Best For**: Localised marketing, seasonal promotions, and targeting niche demographics. Direct mail can be particularly effective for high-end products, home décor, and specialty goods.

Chapter 8 - Summary

To effectively market to South Korean consumers, a well-rounded strategy that includes digital engagement, influencer marketing, and a keen awareness of trends is essential. By leveraging social media, optimising for local search engines, and collaborating with influencers, you can create a dynamic marketing presence that resonates with South Korean consumers. Combining these efforts with traditional marketing methods and personalising your approach based on consumer behaviour and preferences will help build brand loyalty and increase your reach in South Korea's competitive market.

CHAPTER 9: NAVIGATING SOUTH KOREAN BUSINESS ETIQUETTE

South Korean business culture places a high value on respect, hierarchy, and formality. Knowing the expectations around business etiquette is crucial for building trust and credibility with South Korean clients, partners, and customers. This chapter will guide you through the essentials of South Korean business etiquette, including communication styles, meeting conduct, dress codes, and tips for developing long-term business relationships.

9.1 Formality and Respect in Business Interactions

South Korean business culture is characterised by formality and respect, with an emphasis on hierarchy and honour. Understanding these values will help you navigate professional interactions successfully.

Hierarchy and Titles

Hierarchy is a core part of South Korean society and is reflected in the way people interact within a business context. Age and job title play significant roles in determining levels of respect.

- **Using Titles**: When addressing South Korean professionals, use their titles (e.g., Manager Kim, Director Lee) rather than first names. Avoid first names unless you are invited to use them, as this can be perceived as overly informal.

- **Respect for Seniors**: Seniority is highly respected in South Korean business culture. During introductions or meetings, show deference to older or higher-ranking individuals. This can be done through gestures such as waiting for seniors to initiate handshakes or being attentive when they speak.

Politeness and Communication Style

South Korean professionals communicate in a way that is polite, indirect, and respectful. Being mindful of communication styles will help you avoid misunderstandings and build positive relationships.

- **Indirect Communication**: South Koreans often communicate indirectly to avoid causing offence or embarrassment. Rather than saying "no" directly, it is common to express hesitancy or say "we'll consider it." Be mindful of reading between the lines and avoid being too blunt.

- **Active Listening**: Listening carefully without interrupting is essential. Acknowledge others by nodding or using polite verbal affirmations, such as "yes" or "I see," to show engagement.

- **Avoiding Confrontation**: Avoid openly disagreeing or criticising in public settings, as maintaining "face" (dignity and respect) is important. Instead, handle conflicts privately and tactfully.

9.2 Business Meetings and Networking

Punctuality, formality, and structured conduct are important aspects of business meetings in South Korea. Networking events are also valuable opportunities to build trust and establish rapport.

Punctuality

Punctuality is highly valued in South Korean business culture, as it shows respect for others' time. Always aim to arrive on time, or even a few minutes early, for meetings and appointments.

- **Arriving on Time**: Arriving late can be perceived as disrespectful. If you anticipate being delayed, be sure to inform your host or contact ahead of time.

- **Ending Meetings**: Meetings typically end at the scheduled time, as South Korean professionals often have tight schedules. Conclude your discussions promptly and be mindful of overstaying.

Meeting Conduct

South Korean business meetings are generally structured, starting with formal introductions and small talk before moving into the main agenda. Here are some key tips for navigating meetings:

- **Exchanging Business Cards**: The exchange of business cards is an important part of introductions. Offer your card with both hands and receive others' cards with both hands, carefully examining them before putting them away. Keep received cards on the table during the meeting as a sign of respect.

- **Formal Introductions**: Introductions are usually made in order of seniority, with the most senior person introducing themselves first. Use this time to express respect and build rapport with the team.

- **Sticking to the Agenda**: South Korean meetings are often agenda-driven, so stay focused and concise when presenting information. Be prepared with relevant data, and expect to answer detailed questions.

Networking Events

Networking is an essential part of South Korean business culture, and attending networking events can help you establish valuable connections.

- **Business Cards and Contact Information**: Keep a supply of business cards readily available, as they are frequently exchanged at networking events. Be prepared to discuss your role and company, and use this opportunity to follow up with new contacts later.

- **Follow-Up Etiquette**: After networking events, follow

up with an email or message thanking the person for their time and reiterating your interest in potential collaboration. A prompt follow-up is considered courteous and professional.

9.3 Dress Codes in South Korean Business Settings

Business attire in South Korea is formal, conservative, and professional. Adhering to dress codes is a sign of respect and indicates your seriousness in conducting business.

Formal Business Attire

For formal meetings and corporate settings, the dress code is generally conservative, and business attire is preferred.

- **Men's Attire**: Men are typically expected to wear dark suits with ties. Neutral colours such as black, navy, or grey are preferred. Shoes should be polished and formal.
- **Women's Attire**: Women often wear business suits or conservative dresses, keeping accessories minimal. Colours should be subdued, and revealing clothing is generally avoided.

Business Casual

In more relaxed business settings or industries, a business casual dress code may be acceptable. However, it's still best to err on the side of formality unless informed otherwise.

- **Men**: Business casual for men typically includes collared shirts, smart trousers, and a blazer. Ties may not be necessary in less formal environments.
- **Women**: Business casual attire for women may include blouses, tailored trousers, or knee-length skirts. Choose outfits that remain professional and appropriate.

Regional and Industry Variations

In creative or tech industries, the dress code may be more relaxed, with business casual attire more common. Nonetheless, conservative dress is generally preferred, especially for initial meetings.

9.4 Building Long-Term Business Relationships

Building strong relationships is essential to success in South Korea. South Korean professionals prefer to work with people they trust, and establishing this trust can lead to long-lasting business partnerships.

Commitment and Reliability

Reliability is highly valued in South Korean business culture. Consistently meeting deadlines, following through on promises, and delivering high-quality work will help you earn the trust of your South Korean counterparts.

- **Delivering on Promises**: Honour commitments and avoid making promises you cannot keep, as this can harm your credibility. South Koreans respect individuals and companies that are dependable.

- **Consistency**: Building trust takes time, and South Korean professionals are cautious about forming partnerships without consistent proof of reliability. Maintain open lines of communication and update partners on project progress.

Socialising Outside of Business

In South Korea, building relationships outside of formal settings is an important part of business culture. Dinners, social gatherings, and activities are often used to strengthen bonds and get to know business partners on a personal level.

- **Business Meals**: It's common to discuss business over meals. Wait for your host to initiate business talk, as they may prefer to start with casual conversation. Avoid topics such as politics or personal matters unless invited.

- **Drinking Culture**: Drinking, particularly with colleagues, is part of South Korean business culture, and social gatherings often involve alcohol. While participation is appreciated, it is acceptable to politely decline if you do not drink. If you do drink, remember that it's customary to pour drinks for others and accept drinks poured by colleagues as a sign of camaraderie.

- **Gift Giving**: Gift-giving is common in South Korea as a sign of respect and goodwill. Small, thoughtful gifts are appreciated, particularly during holidays like Chuseok or Seollal (Lunar New Year). Avoid overly expensive or extravagant gifts, as this can make recipients uncomfortable.

Respecting Privacy and Personal Space

While building strong relationships is essential, South Korean professionals also value privacy. Respect boundaries and avoid prying into personal matters unless invited.

- **Space and Boundaries**: South Koreans are generally respectful of personal space, so avoid physical contact beyond handshakes unless you're on familiar terms.

- **Professional Distance**: In the initial stages, maintain a respectful distance. As relationships strengthen, South Korean professionals may become more open, but it's crucial to allow them to set the pace.

Chapter 9 - Summary

Navigating South Korean business etiquette involves a blend of respect, formality, and understanding of cultural norms. Building strong relationships requires patience, commitment, and the ability to demonstrate respect for hierarchy and social protocols. By adhering to proper meeting conduct, dressing appropriately, and engaging in social activities, you can build trust and establish credibility with South Korean partners. Remember that long-term success in South Korea is often achieved through reliable, consistent partnerships and a genuine interest in building mutual respect and trust.

CHAPTER 10: CONCLUSION – UNLOCKING SUCCESS IN SOUTH KOREA

South Korea is a dynamic and fast-paced market filled with opportunities for businesses willing to understand and adapt to its unique culture, consumer preferences, and business etiquette. From the thriving e-commerce industry to traditional markets and professional networking, South Korea offers numerous pathways to success for brands and entrepreneurs with the right approach. This chapter summarises the key insights and strategies explored throughout this guide and provides final recommendations for long-term success in the South Korean market.

10.1 Key Takeaways for Travelling and Selling in South Korea

Throughout this guide, we've covered essential aspects of establishing a business presence and selling in South Korea. Below are the most important points to remember as you embark on or continue your journey in this market.

Understanding South Korean Culture and Consumer Behaviour

- South Korean culture combines respect for tradition with a strong embrace of innovation. South Korean consumers are trend-sensitive, quality-conscious, and digitally engaged, making it essential to stay responsive to changes in the market.

- Building a strong brand image that aligns with South Korean values, such as quality, credibility, and innovation, can help you stand out. Pay attention to trends in K-pop, K-beauty, and technology, as these cultural influences heavily impact consumer choices.

Navigating South Korean Logistics and Infrastructure

- South Korea's transport and logistics networks are highly developed, making travel and product delivery efficient and reliable. Use public transport, high-speed trains, and convenient domestic shipping solutions to reach consumers and partners across the country.

- Managing inventory and ensuring timely delivery are crucial, especially for online businesses. Partnering with trusted couriers and offering flexible delivery options like click-and-collect can boost customer satisfaction.

Setting Up a Business with Compliance and Local Insight

- Choose the right business structure to meet your goals, whether it's a sole proprietorship, LLC, or corporation. Register with the appropriate authorities, understand tax obligations, and comply with consumer protection laws, including data protection and product safety.

- South Korea's regulations on advertising, labelling, and consumer rights require careful attention. Transparent business practices and quality customer service are essential for building trust with South Korean consumers.

Leveraging Markets, Fairs, and E-Commerce

- Traditional markets and fairs offer opportunities for businesses selling fashion, crafts, food, and souvenirs, allowing direct engagement with consumers. Choose markets that align with your product and target demographic, and set up an attractive, well-organised stall to capture attention.

- E-commerce is highly popular in South Korea. Use platforms like Coupang, Gmarket, and Naver Smart Store to reach a broad audience, and craft a localised online shopping experience with Korean language options, secure payment methods, and fast delivery.

Effective Marketing Strategies

- Create a multi-channel marketing approach that includes social media, influencer partnerships, and SEO optimised for Naver. Engaging with South Korean consumers on Instagram, KakaoTalk, and YouTube can boost brand visibility and drive sales.

- Traditional marketing methods, such as print ads and outdoor advertising, can also support brand awareness, particularly in busy urban centres. Tailoring your message to South Korean preferences and values will help you connect with a local audience.

Navigating Business Etiquette and Building Relationships

- Respect for hierarchy, formality, and long-term relationships is fundamental in South Korean business culture. Consistency, reliability, and following through on promises are crucial for building trust with South Korean partners.

- Networking and social interactions, including meals and informal gatherings, are essential for building rapport. Be patient, demonstrate respect for cultural norms, and avoid high-pressure tactics to foster positive, lasting relationships.

10.2 Steps to Unlocking Success in South Korea

Below are the key steps to take as you build and grow your business in South Korea.

1. Research and Adapt to the Market

- Understand the regional and seasonal trends in South Korea to tailor your product offerings. Pay attention to consumer demands for quality, convenience, and innovation, and remain adaptable to the rapid changes in this trend-sensitive market.

- Stay updated on South Korean pop culture, consumer behaviour, and industry-specific trends, especially in sectors like fashion, beauty, technology, and food, to ensure your offerings remain relevant and appealing.

2. Establish a Strong, Localised Brand Identity

- Build a brand that resonates with South Korean consumers by emphasising quality, sustainability, and innovation. Tailor your messaging, product presentation, and customer service to the preferences and values of the local market.

- Localise your online presence by using Korean language options, optimising for Naver, and engaging on social media channels popular in South Korea. Position your brand as approachable, professional, and responsive.

3. Build Strong Relationships and Network Consistently

- Invest time in relationship-building with South Korean clients, partners, and suppliers. Attend networking events, participate in industry gatherings, and nurture relationships through consistent, professional interactions.

- Demonstrate reliability by delivering on commitments and communicating transparently. Follow up after meetings and networking events to strengthen your connections and establish long-term partnerships.

4. Prioritise Customer Satisfaction and Trust

- South Korean consumers are discerning and brand-loyal. Providing high-quality products, excellent customer service, and efficient delivery options are key to retaining customers and encouraging repeat purchases.

- Encourage and manage customer reviews, especially on platforms like Naver, Coupang, and KakaoTalk. Positive feedback and trust signals can significantly enhance your brand's credibility.

5. Adapt Your Strategy as You Grow

- As your business gains traction in South Korea, be prepared to refine your strategy based on performance, customer feedback, and market trends. Regularly assess which products and approaches are resonating and adjust your offerings accordingly.

- Continuously engage with your audience through social media, seasonal promotions, and personalised recommendations. Building a brand that is adaptable and in tune with South Korean consumer expectations will help you grow sustainably.

Final Thoughts: Unlocking Your Potential in South Korea

South Korea's vibrant and competitive market presents a wealth of opportunities for businesses willing to adapt and engage with its unique culture. By embracing South Korea's digital landscape, understanding local consumer behaviour, and respecting business etiquette, you can create a brand that stands out and resonates with South Korean consumers. Success in South Korea requires a commitment to quality, consistency, and cultural understanding, and with the right strategies, your brand can thrive in this influential market.

As you move forward, remember that patience, adaptability, and dedication to building genuine relationships are key to long-term success in South Korea. With the insights and strategies from this guide, you are now well-equipped to unlock the potential of the South Korean market and navigate the exciting journey ahead.

Good luck with your venture in South Korea, and may your business flourish as you unlock the opportunities in this dynamic, fast-paced market!

ABOUT THE AUTHOR

J K Lewis

'South Korea Unlocked: A Short Guide to Travelling and Selling in South Korea', is designed to offer useful information and background about South Korea, it's business environment and its culture. The book is aimed towards Entrepreneurs and Sales People as they enter South Korean marketplace with new products and services.